Is It Wet?

By Carmel Reilly

It is wet.

The pots get wet.

The web is wet.

pots

web

Look at Lev.

He is wet!

Pit! Pat!

It is not wet.

It is hot!

Kim gets figs in the sun.

Kim gets a keg.

She pops the figs in the keg.

It is not hot.

It is wet.

See the fog!

Mum and Vic are not wet.

Mum lit the big logs.

It is hot!

The sun is up.

Lin gets her cap and kit.

Lin can see kids at the net.

The kids can hit!

CHECKING FOR MEANING

1. Where does Kim put the figs? *(Literal)*

2. Who lit the big logs? *(Literal)*

3. Why do you think Lin got her cap? *(Inferential)*

EXTENDING VOCABULARY

get	Look at the word *get*. Find a word that rhymes with *get* in the book. What other words do you know that rhyme with *get*?
figs	Say the word *figs*. What sound does the *s* on the end of this word make? What other sound can *s* make?
kit	What does the word *kit* mean in this book? What else can it mean?

MOVING BEYOND THE TEXT

1. What are your favourite things to do when the weather is wet?

2. What is your favourite type of weather? Why?

3. How can you keep warm when the weather is cold? How can you keep cool when it is hot?

4. What is a first-aid kit? What might you find in a first-aid kit?

SPEED SOUNDS

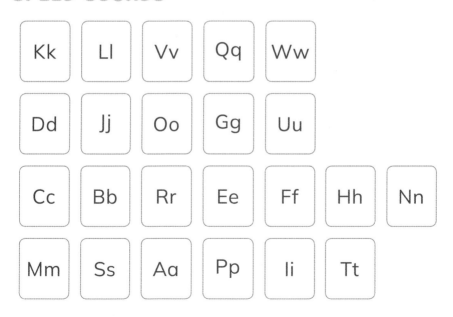

Kk	Ll	Vv	Qq	Ww		
Dd	Jj	Oo	Gg	Uu		
Cc	Bb	Rr	Ee	Ff	Hh	Nn
Mm	Ss	Aa	Pp	Ii	Tt	

PRACTICE WORDS

wet

Kim

web

Lev

keg

Vic

lit

kit

Lin

logs

kids